FOR THOSE WHO WORK

Stations of the Cross

Ordinary Mysteries of the Rosary

meditations by
Stanley J. Konieczny

and
Gregory F. Augustine Pierce

drawings by
Jean Morman Unsworth

ACTA Publications
Chicago, Illinois

FOR THOSE WHO WORK
Stations of the Cross
Ordinary Mysteries of the Rosary

Meditations on the Stations of the Cross
 by Stanley J. Konieczny
Meditations on the Ordinary Mysteries of the Rosary
 by Gregory F. Augustine Pierce

Drawings by Jean Morman Unsworth

Design by John Dylong
Typesetting by LINK Book Development and Production

Scripture selections are taken from THE NEW AMERICAN BIBLE, copyright © 1970 Confraternity of Christian Doctrine, Washington, D.C. and are used with permission. All rights reserved.

Quotations from papal documents are taken from various editions published by the Daughters of St. Paul and are edited for clarity and inclusive language.

Copyright © 1991 ACTA Publications
4848 N. Clark Street
Chicago, Illinois 60640
312-271-1030

All rights reserved. No part of this publication may be reproduced or transmitted in any form or by any means, electronic or mechanical, including photocopying and recording, or by any information storage and retrieval system, without permission in writing from ACTA Publications.

Library of Congress Catalogue Card Number: 90-085660
ISBN: 0-87946-053-9

Printed in the United States of America

Contents

Preface 5

The Stations of the Cross 9

The Ordinary Mysteries of the Rosary . . . 73

FOR THOSE WHO WORK

Preface

To him whose power now at work in us can do immeasurably more than we ask or imagine—to him be glory in the church and in Christ Jesus through all generations, world without end. Amen.
Ephesians 3:20–21

The connection between work and prayer has not always been clear to the average Christian. In many ways, prayer and meditation have been seen as "getting away from" the ordinary, the mundane, the tiring, the difficult activities of the workaday world. Work, on the other hand, has been considered by many to be a burden, a curse, the "sweat of your brow" promised to Adam and Eve (and their descendants) as a punishment for the original sin.

No matter what our occupation happens to be, however, work is a dominant factor in our lives, even if only by virtue of the amount of our waking time invested in it. Work—both paid and unpaid—provides us with some of our most rewarding and fulfilling moments. Work can also pose some of the most serious problems in our lives. We can find both support and challenge for the way we understand and perform our work in two traditional devotions of the Church: the Stations (or Way) of the Cross and the Mysteries of the Rosary.

For centuries, these two spiritual exercises have been a source of comfort and insight to Christians. The Stations are found in virtually every Catholic church, and retracing—alone or with others—the footsteps of Jesus in his passion and death remains an excellent way to reflect on the meaning of his redemptive act in our lives. With the Rosary, the soothing repetition of the Our Father, ten Hail Marys, and the Glory Be, combined with meditation on incidents in the life of the Holy Family, has made it a prayer accessible to all yet adaptable to each.

Unfortunately, the Stations and the Rosary have fallen out of use with many people precisely because they have become so familiar. Countless repetitions may have drained these devotions of some of their power and meaning. The reflections in *For Those Who Work* are an attempt to renew these practices by connecting them directly with our daily work on our jobs, with our families, and in our communities and churches.

> Life is built up every day from work; from work it derives its specific dignity, but at the same time work contains the unceasing measure of human toil and suffering, and also of the harm and injustice, which penetrate deeply into social life within individual nations and on the international level.
> John Paul II
> *On Human Work*

THE STATIONS OF THE CROSS

Introduction

Anyone who does not take up his cross and follow me cannot be my disciple.
                                                    Luke 14:27

Christ's passion and death did not take place in a vacuum. Jesus carried his cross through the marketplace of his day. Salvation for all humanity was realized in the narrow, winding streets of Jerusalem—streets crammed with merchants and vendors, lawyers and philosophers, shoppers and pickpockets. Many people working that day let the saviour of the world pass by them on his way to Calvary, too busy to give him so much as a second glance.

He may have stumbled before a small shop where a butcher's heavy thumb was weighed in among the lamb chops. Perhaps he met his mother within earshot of two contractors bickering over how they should complete some construction project. As the Roman guards beat and prodded him along, some master craftsman most likely was verbally lashing out at an apprentice over a petty mistake.

Jesus of Nazareth still carries his cross through the marketplace: the offices, the conference rooms, the banks, the schoolrooms, the hospitals, the shopping malls. He trudges over fields plowed for spring planting and into mines, factories, rail yards, loading docks and airports. Do we ever notice him there, or are we too distracted by the business at hand? Do we help him carry his cross or do we put extra pressure on his shoulders? Do we give witness to him or deny we ever knew the man?

These Stations of the Cross are designed to help us follow Jesus on his way through the marketplace. We will discover new meaning in our daily work as we evaluate our actions in light of the gospel and the Church's teachings.

> Jesus Christ, by his "plentiful redemption" has by no means taken away the various tribulations with which mortal life is interwoven, but has so clearly transformed them into incentives to virtue and sources of merit that no mortal can attain eternal reward unless he follows the blood-stained footsteps of Jesus Christ.
>
> Leo XIII
> *Rerum Novarum*

I

Pilate Condemns Jesus to Death

So Pilate, who wished to satisfy the crowd, released Barabbas to them; and after he had had Jesus scourged, he handed him over to be crucified.
                                               Mark 15:15

A man of position, Pontius Pilate sacrificed the life of another to safeguard that position. Motivated by fear, Pilate bowed to social and political pressures. The public official found himself caught in a power play and reacted by compromising what he knew to be right.

Standing in spirit with you, Jesus, before Pilate's judicial bench, I reflect on how I make decisions at my work during the course of the day. What standard do I use in determining my actions? Do I act according to your commandments of love of God and love of neighbor, or do I gauge my efforts against the ladder of success? Do I see my career as an opportunity for service, or am I engaged in a game in which my every move is part of a strategy to win? Am I motivated primarily by your teachings or by the approval of my co-workers and supervisors? On what values do I make my decisions?

Lord Jesus, crucified, have mercy on me.

> The Church's teaching has always expressed the strong and deep conviction that human work concerns not only the economy, but also, and especially, personal values. The economic system itself and the production process benefit precisely when these personal values are fully respected.
>
> John Paul II
> *Laborem Exercens*

II

Jesus Takes Up His Cross

Jesus was led away, and carrying the cross by himself, went out to what is called the Place of the Skull (in Hebrew Golgotha).

John 19:16–17

Jesus must have staggered under the weight of the cross as it was placed on his shoulders. Surely he had often hauled beams like this as a carpenter, but this wood was different. Instead of being the raw material for tables, chests and chairs—for things of life—this wood was utilized for destruction. Only God's great love brought life to this instrument of death.

Jesus, I can identify with you as you take up your cross. Sometimes it seems that I wake up tired—weary of the heavy crosses I am expected to bear of routine, responsibility, and regeneration. Give me the grace to accept the difficulties which I encounter in my work. Remind me that I am also quite capable of laying crosses on my co-workers' shoulders. I can weigh others down with my expectations, unrealistic goals, prejudices, and pettiness. In the name of getting the job done, I can pile work on others and then poke and prod them toward the deadline. Forgive me, Lord, for the times when I am a cross to others.

Lord Jesus, crucified, have mercy on me.

> By enduring the toil of work in union with Christ crucified for us, we in a way collaborate with the Son of God for the redemption of humanity. We show ourselves to be true disciples of Christ by carrying the cross in his turn every day in the activity that we are called upon to perform.
>
> John Paul II
> *Laborem Exercens*

III

Jesus Falls the First Time

Have pity on me, O Lord, for I am in distress; with sorrow my eye is consumed; my soul also, and my body. For my life is spent with grief and my years with sighing.

Psalm 31:10–11

The abuse, the anxiety, the weight of the cross drained Jesus and sent him crashing to the pavement. Perhaps he just needed one brief moment to recover, but the soldiers kept pushing him forward. The hecklers in the mob shouted their taunts. The entire ordeal had robbed him of his energy. He fell, but then he got up again and continued.

Jesus, your stumbling and falling showed me that you understand how I feel sometimes. So often, work leaves me physically and spiritually drained. The overtime, the deadlines, the demands of supervisors, customers, and co-workers seem to sap every ounce of my energy—leaving me tired, lifeless, and—yes—sometimes bitter. When I feel as though I am completely used up, help me to find strength and renewal in you. Then I will be able to pick up my share of the load and struggle onward.

Lord Jesus, crucified, have mercy on me.

> Individuals, families and nations, be they poor or rich, can be overcome by avarice, and all can fall victim to stifling materialism. Increased possession is not the ultimate goal of nations nor of individuals. All growth is ambivalent.
>
> Paul VI
> *Populorum Progressio*

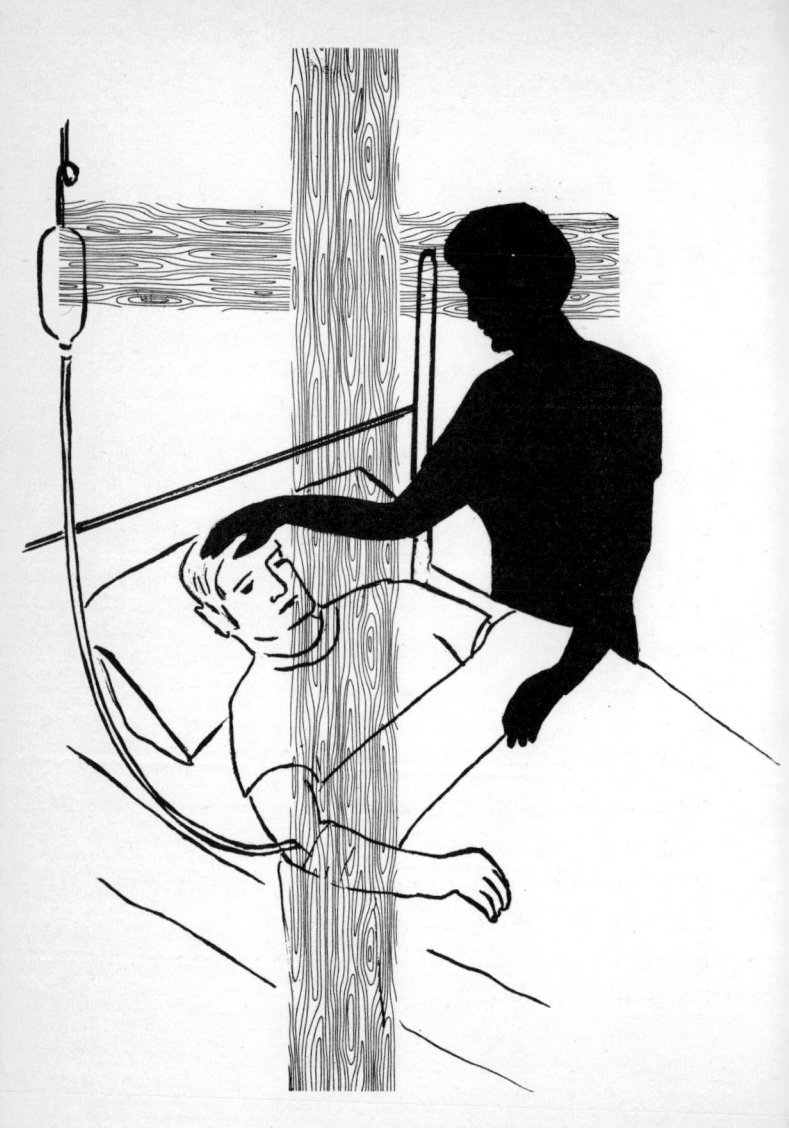

IV

Jesus Meets His Mother

These are my mother and my brothers. Whoever does the will of God is brother and sister and mother to me.

Mark 3:34–35

The guards cleared a path for Jesus through the crowd. In the midst of the multitude of faces—some livid with hate, others blank with indifference—Jesus spotted that one face that meant so much to him. His eyes made contact with his mother's. Mary had remained her son's faithful disciple to the end, sharing in his loneliness and rejection as no other could have done. She reminds us of how God works in our lives. From the poor stable of Bethlehem through exile in Egypt to the hill country of Galilee, Mary's "yes" to the Lord had led her on an odyssey of love and faith that brought her to the foot of the cross.

Jesus, am I faithful the way Mary was? Do I say "yes" to God every day as I go about my daily work? Do my beliefs influence the way I respond to those with whom I work? Do I act any differently because I am your follower?

Lord Jesus, crucified, have mercy on me.

> She is held up as an example to the faithful for the way in which, in her own particular life, she fully and responsibly accepted the will of God, because she heard the word of God and acted on it, and because charity and a spirit of service were the driving force of her actions. She is worthy of imitation because she was the first and most perfect of Christ's disciples.
>
> Paul VI
> *Marialis Cultus*

V

Simon Helps Jesus Carry His Cross

A man named Simon of Cyrene, the father of Alexander and Rufus, was coming in from the fields, and they pressed him into service to carry the cross.
                                               Mark 15:21

What next? That question of desperation must have summed up Simon's feelings as he was ordered to help Jesus carry the cross. After all, Simon had his own concerns. As a farmer, he worried about crops and weather and problems with his soil. As a family man, he felt the weight of responsibilities at home. Now, somebody else needed him—someone he didn't even know. How could he refuse? Would he dare refuse?

Jesus, often I feel like Simon. So many demands press upon me. My job consumes more and more of my time, talent and energy. Although I am drained by quitting time, I know that I owe my interest and attention to my family, to my church, to my community, to my friends—and yes, even to strangers. I feel overwhelmed at times by all the responsibilities that tug at me day after day. Please give me the grace to give of myself, even when I don't think I can give any more.

Lord Jesus, crucified, have mercy on me.

> More than any other, the individual who is animated by true charity labors skillfully to discover the causes of misery, to find the means to combat it, to overcome it resolutely.
>
> Paul VI
> *Populorum Progressio*

VI

Veronica Wipes the Face of Jesus

And I promise you that whoever gives a cup of cold water to one of these lowly ones because he is a disciple will not want for his reward.
                                    Matthew 10:42

Tradition holds that en route to Calvary Jesus was helped by a woman named Veronica. The story is that this brave woman elbowed her way through the crowd in order to wipe the face of the master. Her act embodied all of Jesus' teachings on charity, and since that day countless Christians have followed in Veronica's footsteps by reaching out in some small—but often courageous—way to those who suffer. Just as Jesus is believed to have left the image of his face on Veronica's veil, so too is every act of kindness marked by his love.

It is easy to feel powerless in the working world, Jesus. I face people and situations that I label impossible and at times it just does not seem as though I can make a difference. Teach me to see, Lord, that although I cannot always change things, I can at least try to make them a little more bearable for everyone. In the spirit of Veronica, I hope I can ease painful situations in the workplace with a sincere smile or a gentle word. Let me always respond to the fellow human being beneath the appearances. Give me the strength and sensitivity to offer a little comfort and help—even if I have to muscle my way through the mob to do so.

Lord Jesus, crucified, have mercy on me.

> It is evident that both the solidarity of the human race and the sense of brotherhood and sisterhood which accords with Christian principles require that some people lend others energetic help in many ways.
>
> John XXIII
> *Mater et Magistra*

VII

Jesus Falls a Second Time

For all my foes I am an object of reproach, a laughingstock to my neighbors, and a dread to my friends; they who see me abroad flee from me.
                                    Psalm 31:12

Jesus must have felt an incredible loneliness on his way to Golgotha. The streets were filled with shoppers preparing for the Sabbath, yet he was utterly alone. Some who had cried "hosanna" on Sunday turned on him on Friday. Perhaps a woman who once sought his healing help now lingered at a merchant's stall studying a piece of cloth that she never intended to buy, just so she would not have to look at him. A young man, who had sat spellbound as he taught, might now have ducked down an alley so he could avoid seeing him.

Jesus, it is still a lonely journey to bear your cross in the marketplace. In fact, it can be almost impossible to live Christian principles there. To distance myself from gossip, off-color jokes, power plays, less-than-honest business practices is difficult and at times I fail. How often have I looked the other way or tried to disassociate myself from someone in need or in trouble? I find it difficult to keep trying—until I remember that you got up and continued on.

Lord Jesus, crucified, have mercy on me.

> When people are motivated by Christian charity, they cannot but love others, and regard the needs, sufferings and joys of others as their own. Their work, wherever it be, is constant, adaptable, humane and has concern for the needs of others.
>
> John XXIII
> *Mater et Magistra*

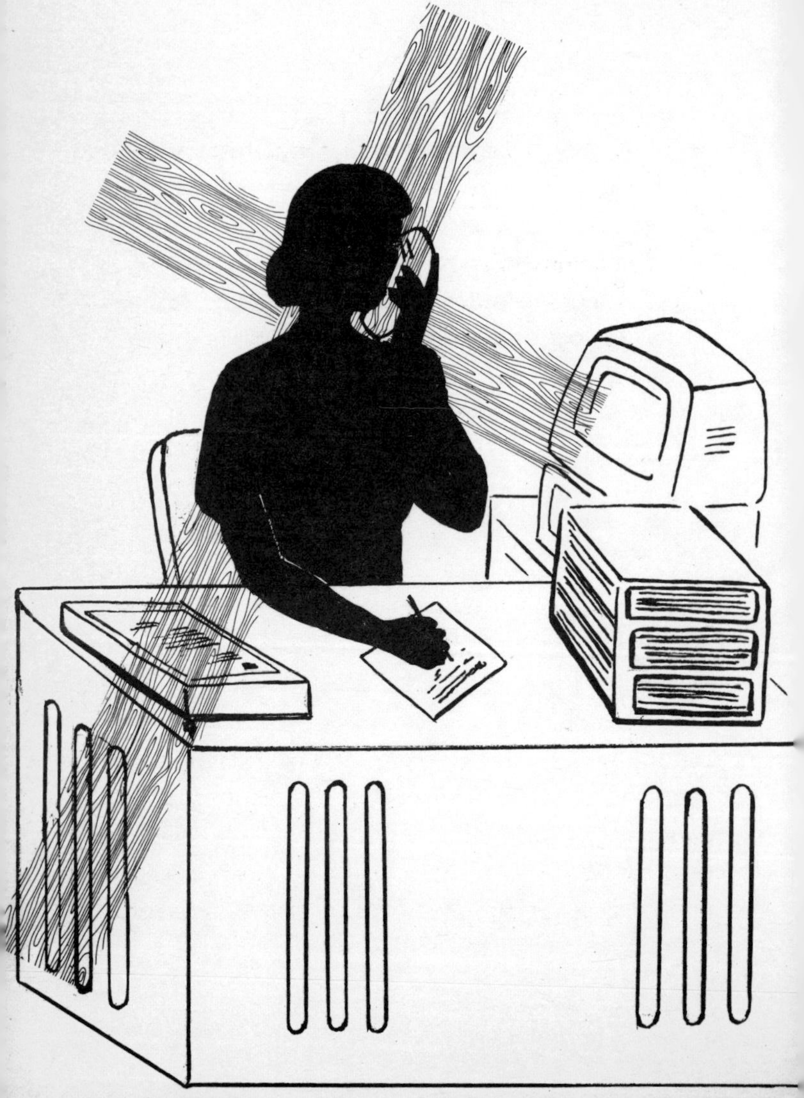

VIII

Jesus Talks with the Women

A great crowd of people followed him, including women who beat their breasts and lamented over him. Jesus turned to them and said, "Daughters of Jerusalem, do not weep for me. Weep for yourselves and for your children."

Luke 23:27–28

Along the way, Jesus saw the women. He heard in their cry a longing for something that might help them make sense out of the nightmare they were witnessing. They sought a word of comfort, a second of kindness in a world overrun with cruelty. Ever the teacher, Jesus found even in the midst of his own suffering a teachable moment to call people one more time to selfless love. His voice may have been softer than usual because of his pain and fatigue, yet there was only mercy in his words.

I imagine your encounter with these women, Jesus, and try to compare the scene with my interactions at work. Facing a deadline, I snap at my co-workers; enduring a tedious routine, I act annoyed with my customers or clients; trying to finish a project, I am curt to a secretary or a delivery person. Help me to remember that even on the way to death you treated others with respect and gentleness.

Lord Jesus, crucified, have mercy on me.

> Justice demands that the dignity of human personality be respected. . . . It is shameful and inhuman to use human beings as things of gain and to put no more value on them than what they are worth in muscle and energy.
>
> Leo XIII
> *Rerum Novarum*

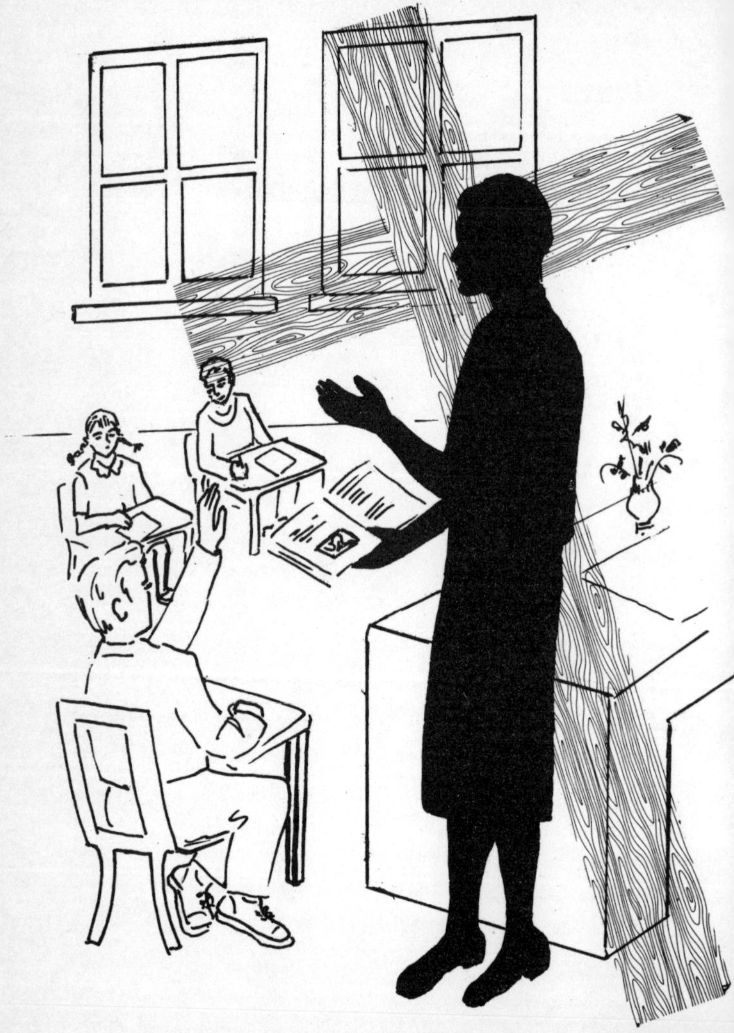

IX

Jesus Falls a Third Time

I hear the whispers of the crowd, that frighten me from every side, as they consult together against me, plotting to take my life.

Psalm 31:14

Again Jesus crumbled beneath his cross. Cobblestones tore at his knees, the course debris of the gutter rubbed roughly against his cheek, wood splinters ripped his shoulder. The physical pain must have been terrible, but perhaps he suffered most from the verbal abuse of the crowd as they cursed him, mocked him, and uttered smug judgments about him. Yet he said nothing.

Jesus, remind me to watch what I say on the job. Help me to remember that words can be either lashes which flay another's self-respect or healing rewards that offer encouragement for a job well done. I can devastate another so easily with undue criticism or undermine morale so simply with thoughtless gossip. My words can either bring fellow workers down low or lift them up at just the right time. A simple statement of gratitude or recognition from me can change the course of someone's day or even career. Teach me, Lord, to build up others rather than knock them down.

Lord Jesus, crucified, have mercy on me.

> People are experiencing a new loneliness; it is not in the face of a hostile nature which it has taken them centuries to subdue, but in an anonymous crowd which surrounds them and in which they feel themselves to be strangers.
>
> Paul VI
> *Octogesima Adveniens*

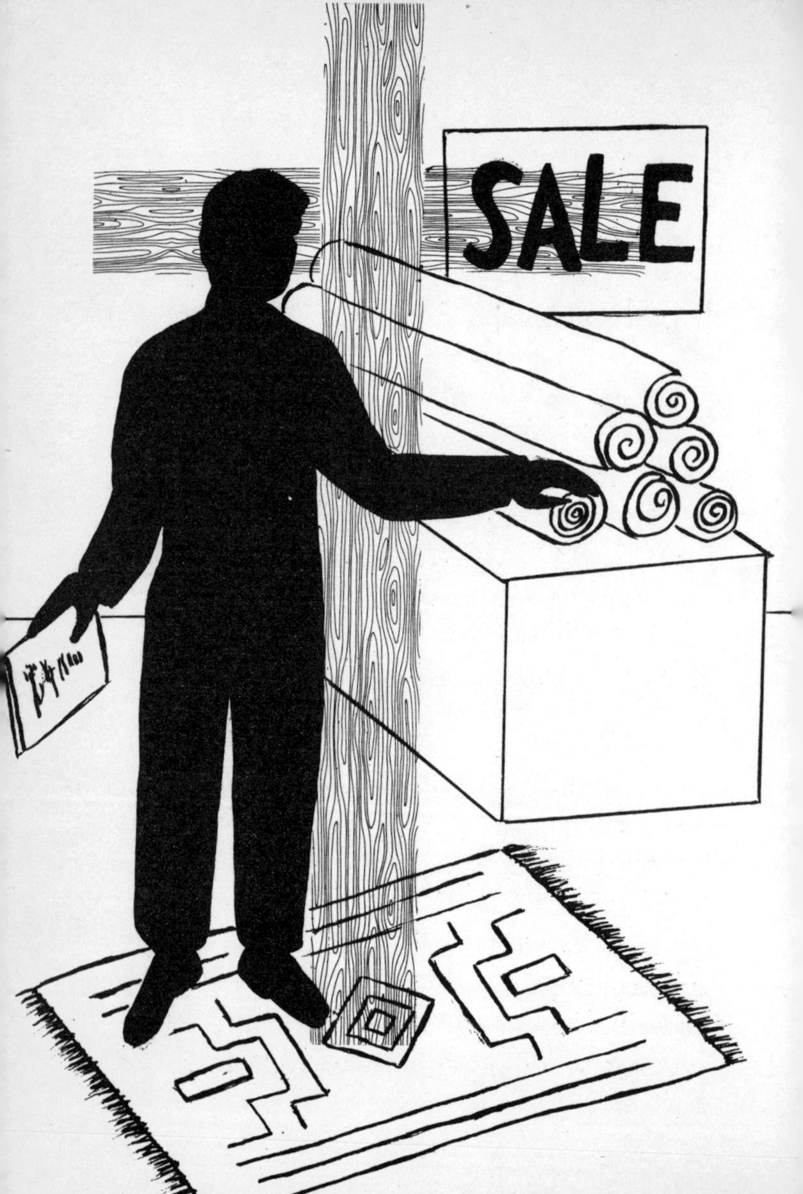
SALE

X

Jesus Is Stripped of His Garments

After the soldiers had crucified Jesus they took his garments and divided them four ways, one for each soldier. There was also his tunic, but this tunic was woven in one piece from top to bottom and had no seam. They said to each other, "We should not tear it. Let us throw dice to see who gets it."

John 19: 23–24

Jesus was born in poverty and died in poverty. As the soldiers tore the very clothes off of his back, they robbed him of the last things he owned in this world. He was left with nothing material. Yet Jesus was unchanged. With no possessions, he still maintained his dignity and identity. He proved himself to be a man of prayer, a man of compassion, a man of forgiveness, a man of healing.

Jesus, I am constantly bombarded by messages which tell me that I am what I own. I am urged to fulfill myself by acquiring more and more things. I am tempted to gauge my success or failure in terms of commissions and overtime, raises and promotions, status symbols and buying power. Yet you have shown me that I am more than my material possessions. Help me to control the consumerism in my life and work.

Lord Jesus, crucified, have mercy on me.

> Too often in our day is verified the testimony of the psalmist concerning worshipers of false gods, namely, human beings in their activity very frequently neglect themselves, but admire their own works as if these were gods: "Their idols are silver and gold; the handiwork of human beings."
>
> John XXIII
> *Mater et Magistra*

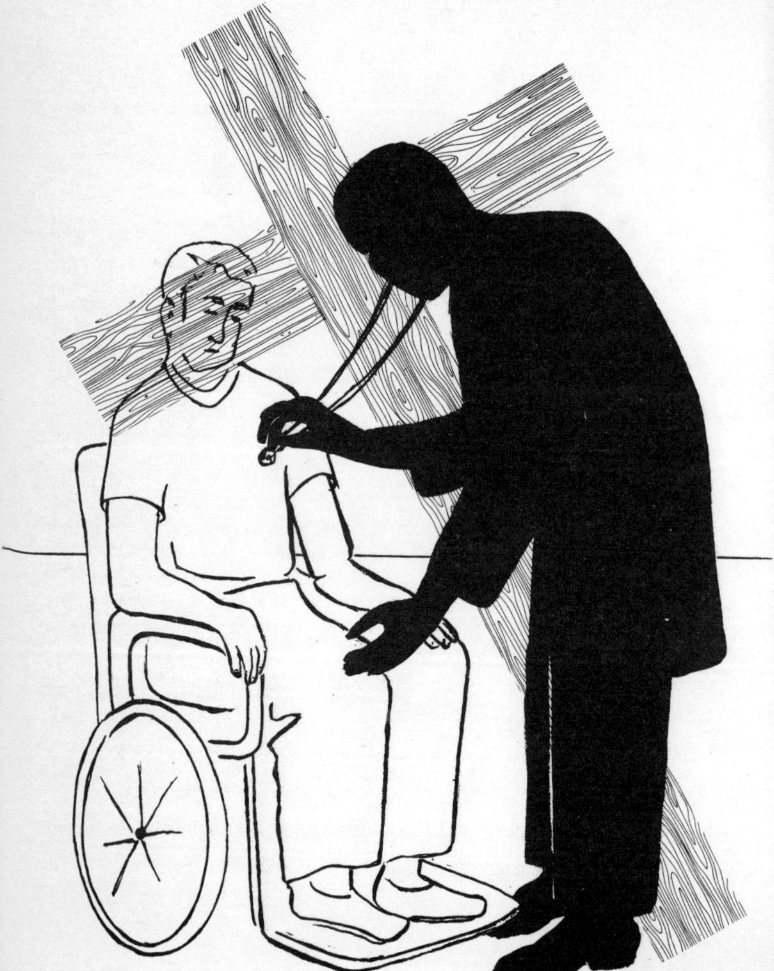

XI

Jesus Is Nailed to the Cross

This is the plan proposed for the whole earth and this the hand outstretched over all nations.
                                               Isaiah 14:26

The prophets often used the image of an outstretched hand to describe the wrath of God. The outstretched hand of God demanded justice and promised punishment and retribution. Jesus created a new image on Calvary. As he stretched out his hands—allowing his executioners to nail them to the cross—he dispensed mercy and salvation, not judgment.

Jesus, the marketplace is full of such stock phrases as "dog eat dog" and "look out for number one." Is my workday motivated by these standards of survival? Do I reach out my hand only to grab more than my co-workers? Do I lift my hand to exercise my own brand of justice upon someone whom I believe has wronged me? Do I ever extend my hand to pat someone on the back, to help raise someone from the depths of depression, or to seek forgiveness with a handshake? Lord, let my hands follow the example of yours and offer love to others in my workplace.

Lord Jesus, crucified, have mercy on me.

> Certainly, the well-being which is so longed for is chiefly to be expected from an abundant outpouring of charity; of Christian charity, we mean, which is in epitome the law of the Gospel, and which, always ready to sacrifice itself for the benefit of others, is humankind's surest antidote against the insolence of the world and immoderate love of self. . . .
>
> Leo XIII
> *Rerum Novarum*

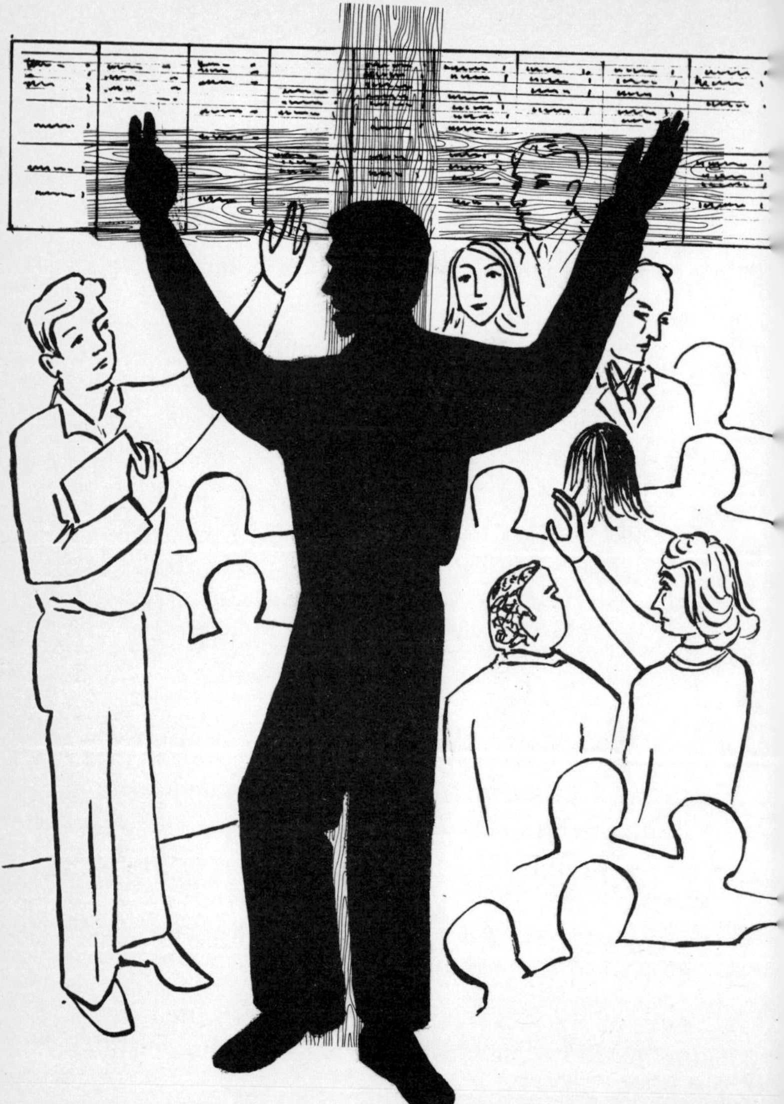

XII

Jesus Dies on the Cross

At that time Jesus cried in a loud voice, "Eloi, Eloi, lama sabachthani?" which means, "My God, My God, why have you forsaken me?" A few of the bystanders who heard it remarked "Listen! He is calling on Elijah!" Someone ran off, and soaking a sponge in sour wine, stuck it on a reed to try to make him drink. The man said, "Now let's see whether Elijah comes to take him down."

Mark 15:34–36

Despite the abuse and the slow, agonizing death by suffocation, Jesus's only complaint on the cross was thirst. His words echoed the psalmist: "My throat is dried up like baked clay. . . ." Jesus wanted just a touch of cool water to ease his pain. Instead they brought him sour wine to keep him alive a little longer so they could satisfy their curiosity. Maybe that is what ultimately killed him: he looked to others for one small act of human kindness, and all he received was one more act of selfishness.

I share your prayer on the cross, Jesus. I, too, thirst. At times I am so weary of my work. I need refreshment, fulfillment, comfort. Unlike you, however, I sometimes accept the sour wine and drink deeply of its temporary satisfaction. I slake my thirst with money, possessions, power. Yet, like the woman at the well, I thirst for living water, Lord. Help me find it through giving rather than taking.

Christ Jesus, crucified, have mercy on me.

There are those who, although professing to be Christians, are almost completely unmindful of that sublime law of justice and charity that binds us not only to render to others what is theirs but to succor brothers and sisters in need as Christ the Lord himself, and—what is worse—out of greed for gain do not scruple to exploit the workers.

Pius XI
Quadragesimo Anno

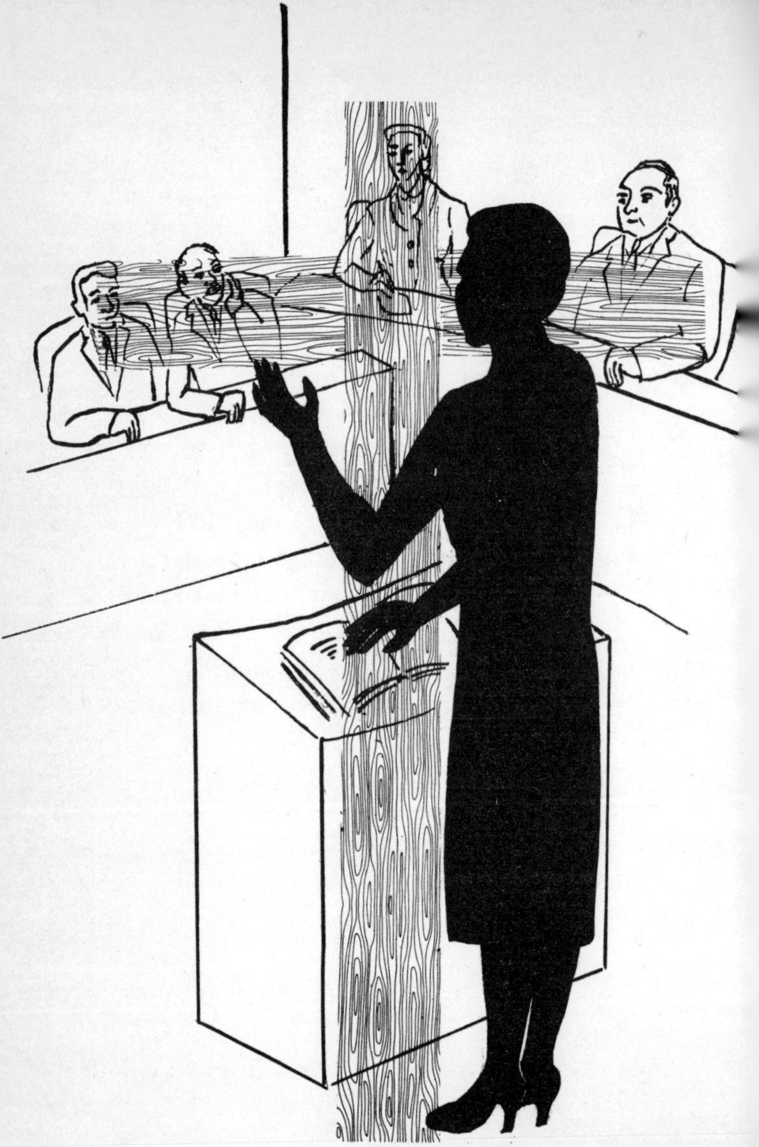

XIII

Jesus Is Placed in the Arms of His Mother

Simeon blessed them and said to Mary, his mother: "This child is destined to be the downfall and the rise of many in Israel, a sign that will be opposed—and you yourself shall be pierced with a sword—so that the thoughts of many hearts may be laid bare."

Luke 2:34–35

The totality of Simeon's prophecy became real to Mary as she cradled the lifeless body of her son. She and a few others had remained as silent witnesses to Jesus' sacrifice of salvation. For what she must have believed was the last time, the mother embraced her son, and in doing so she embraced the cross and all the suffering it entailed in her own life.

Your mother was much more courageous than I, Jesus. I fear the weakness and vulnerability of the cross could spell occupational suicide for me, and so I cling to it only as a concept, a symbol, an ornament. Seldom do I willingly embrace the cross of sacrifice and self-giving in my life and work, for then I might be taken advantage of or used. Yet there is always Mary's example to give me the strength to truly become your follower.

Lord Jesus, crucified, have mercy on me.

> No one has experienced, to the same degree as the mother of the crucified one, the mystery of the cross, the overwhelming encounter of divine transcendent justice with love: that "kiss" given by mercy to justice.
>
> John Paul II
> *Dives in Misericordia*

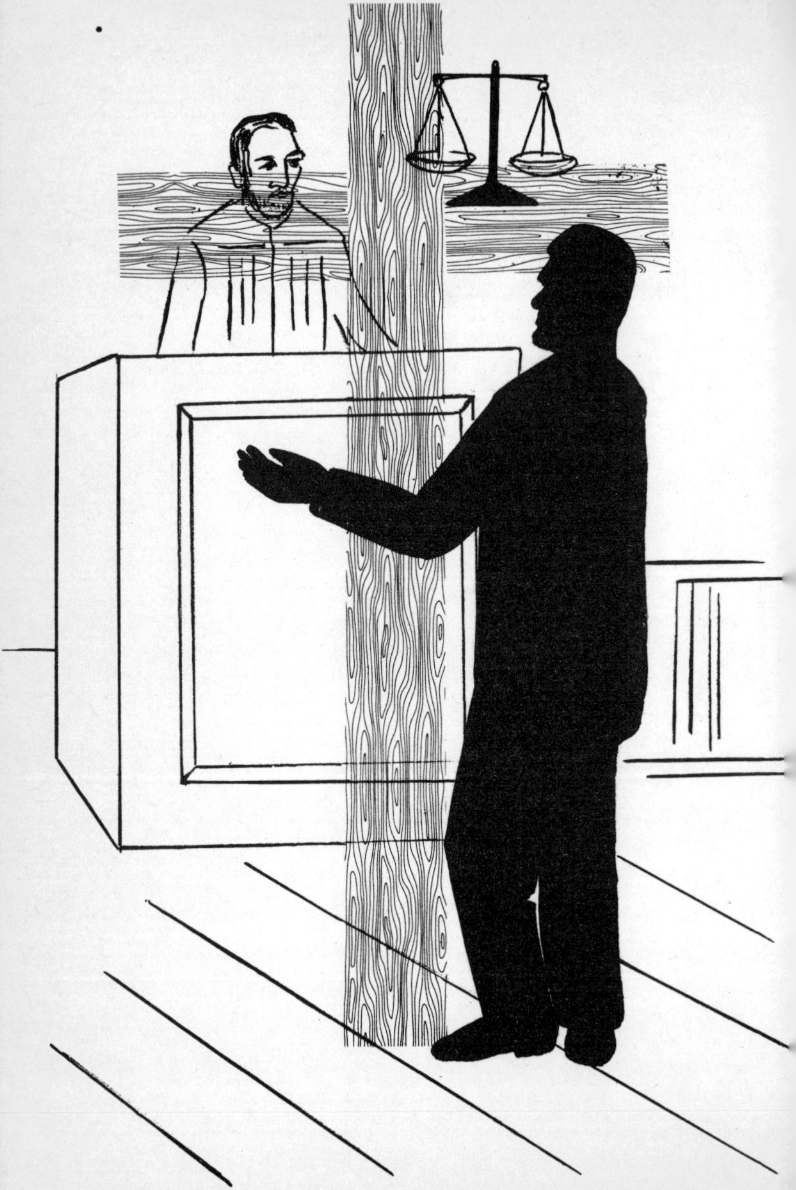

XIV

Jesus Is Laid in the Tomb

Afterward, Joseph of Arimathea, a disciple of Jesus (although a secret one for fear of the Jews), asked Pilate's permission to remove Jesus' body. . . . In the place where he had been crucified there was a garden, and in the garden a new tomb in which no one had ever been buried. Because of the Jewish Preparation Day they buried Jesus there, for the tomb was close at hand.

John 19:38,41–42

Joseph of Arimathea belonged to the "establishment" of his day. He was a professional, perhaps a businessman or a lawyer—definitely a man of learning, status, and wealth. All of these things may have distanced him from Jesus and his message. Joseph believed, but he did not act—until it was "too late." Perhaps he knew that openly following Jesus would have jeopardized his power and prestige, yet the love he witnessed on Calvary finally overcame his fear and allowed him to bravely profess his discipleship—even to Pilate, the man who had condemned Jesus to death.

Jesus, I see some similarities between Joseph and me in my day-to-day dealings with the world. It appears at times that I, too, am a secret disciple for fear of losing my place in the system. I am terrified that by behaving like one of your followers I will diminish my stock in the eyes of others. So I laugh at the racist or sexist joke, jockey for the best position, work to the minimum standards. Let your example help me bury my fear and give me the courage to do what is right.

Lord Jesus, crucified, have mercy on me.

> All of us experience firsthand the sad effects of this blind submission to pure consumerism: in the first place a crass materialism, and at the same time a radical dissatisfaction because one quickly learns—unless one is shielded from the flood of publicity and ceaseless and tempting offers of products—that the more one possesses the more one wants, while deeper aspirations remain unsatisfied and perhaps even stifled.
>
> John Paul II
> *Solicitudo Rei Socialis*

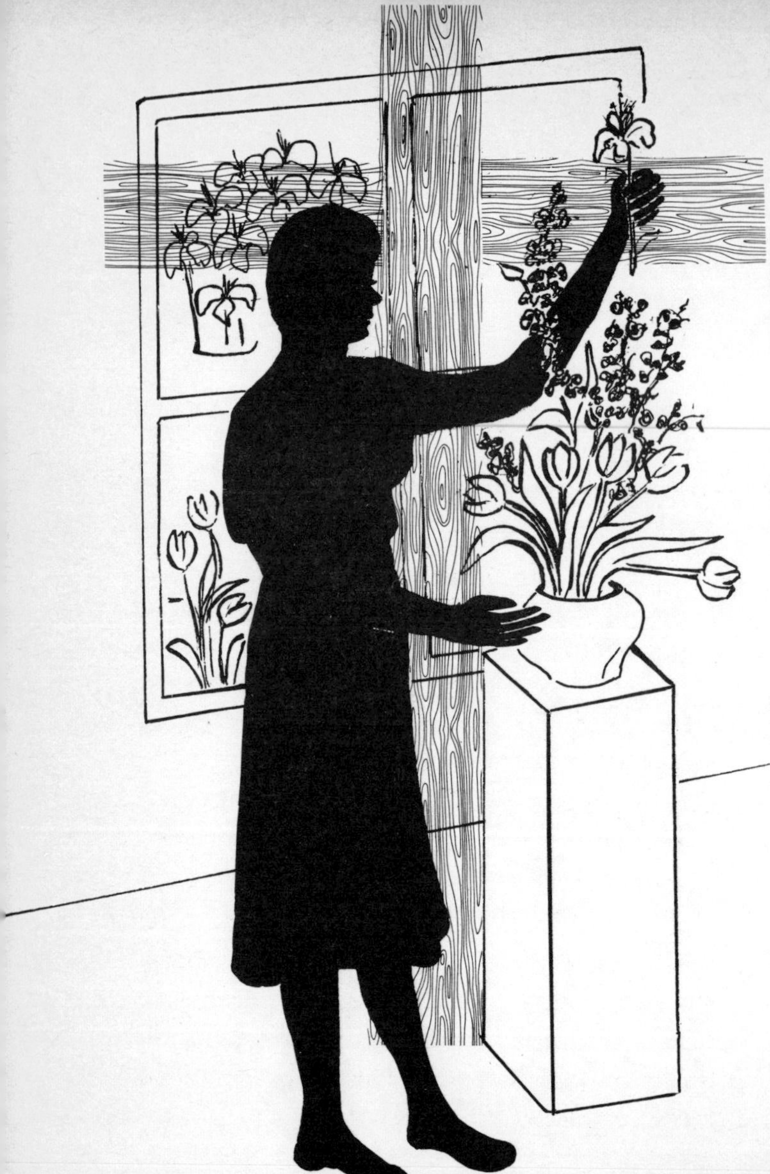

Jesus Is Raised from the Dead

She turned around and caught sight of Jesus standing there. But she did not know him. "Woman," he asked her, "why are you weeping? Who is it you are looking for?" She supposed he was the gardener, so she said, "Sir, if you are the one who carried him off, tell me where you have laid him and I will take him away." Jesus said to her, "Mary!" She turned to him and said in Hebrew, "Rabbouni!" (meaning "Teacher").

John 20:14–16

What did Mary Magdalene see in the garden on that first Easter morning? Not a disembodied spirit or an apparition in flowing robes. Through her tears, she perceived a gardener, a workman. Perhaps it was Jesus' strong build, developed by his years as a carpenter. Or maybe he stooped to smell a flower or touch a clump of olives, some gesture that communicated the nurturing spirit of a farmer. When Magdalene finally recognized Jesus, it was as her teacher.

Jesus, I am glad that Mary Magdalene took you for a worker. This lends a special dignity to my work and that of all who labor. Her beautiful "mistake" in identity has a prophetic quality, as if to tell us that the risen Lord can be encountered in our daily work. Lord, help me to proclaim the good news of our salvation on my job, with my family, and in my community and church. Let me work as I believe.

Lord Jesus, crucified, have mercy on me.

> The Christian finds in human work a small part of the Cross of Christ and accepts it in the same spirit of redemption in which Christ accepted his Cross for us. In work, thanks to the light that penetrates us from the Resurrection of Christ, we always find a glimmer of new life, of the new good, as if it were an announcement of the "new heavens and the new earth" in which humans and the world participate precisely through the toil that goes with work.
>
> John Paul II
> *Laborem Exercens*

THE ORDINARY MYSTERIES OF THE ROSARY

Introduction

*His mother kept all these things in her memory.
Jesus, for his part, progressed steadily in wisdom
and age and grace before God and men.*
                              Luke 2:51–52

The things that Mary and Joseph pondered were not just the miraculous events of their son's life. Jesus did not just learn theology and philosophy from them, but the skills of everyday living. The Holy Family prayed and wondered over the same questions that Christians ask today: How does God act in my daily life? What are the spiritual dimensions of ordinary events?

Holiness, or wholeness, comes from integrating the various spheres of our lives: our work around the home, our jobs outside the home, our community and church involvement. The Rosary can be an excellent means for achieving such holiness. By reflecting on the daily lives of Jesus, Mary and Joseph, we can gain insight and inspiration into our own situations.

Mary, the homemaker, can help us see that God is present in both the exciting and the mundane aspects of that most important of vocations. St. Joseph, the carpenter, gives us an example of competence in work and faithfulness to duty. Jesus, the teacher, spent thirty years of his life in the same normal circumstances that we spend our lives, teaching us how to grow "in wisdom and age and grace."

The Ordinary Mysteries of the Rosary are a contemporary addition to the traditional Joyful, Sorrowful and Glorious Mysteries. They are specifically designed for prayer and reflection on the daily tasks of workaday life, which for most of us include making a living, raising a family, being a good citizen, practicing religion, and balancing these responsibilities.

> On many occasions our predecessors have recommended the frequent recitation of the Rosary ... and recalled its intrinsic effectiveness for promoting Christian life and apostolic commitment.
>
> Paul VI
> *Marialis Cultus*

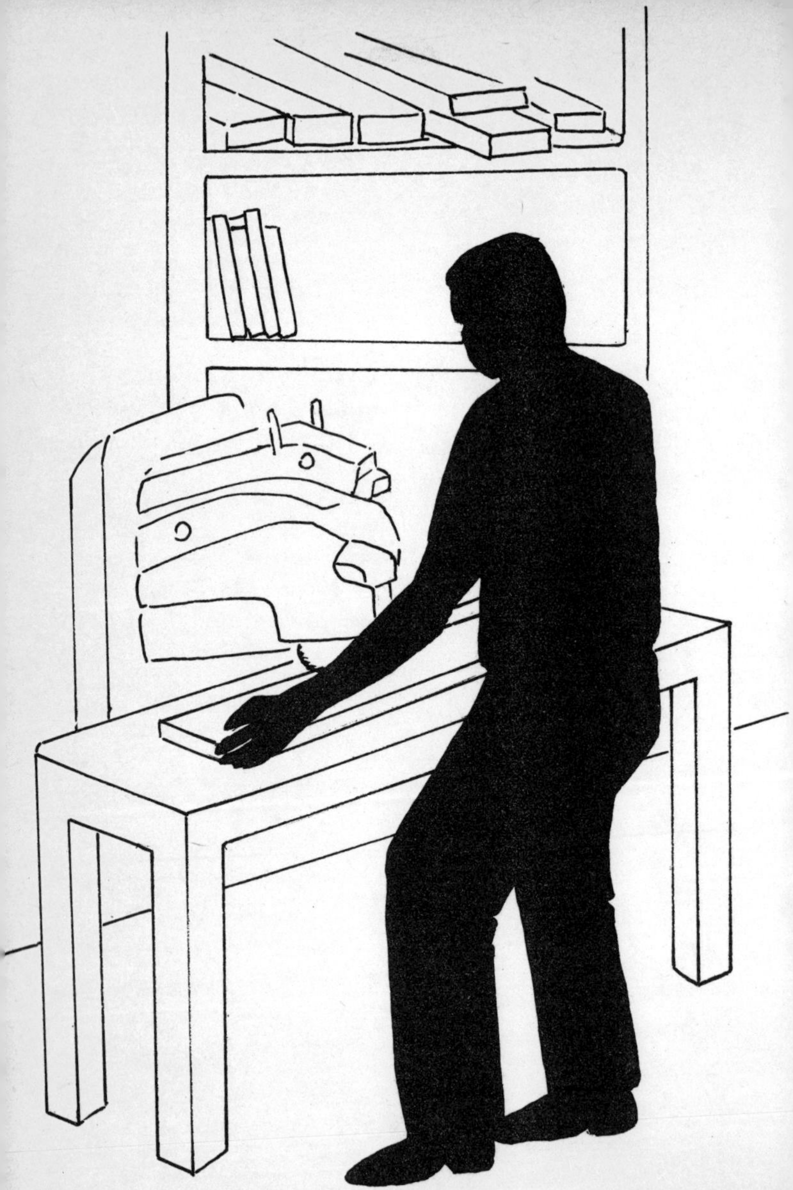

1

Making a Living

Jesus next went to his native place and spent his time teaching them in their synagogue. They were filled with amazement, and said to one another, "Where did this man get such wisdom and miraculous powers? Isn't this the carpenter's son? Isn't Mary known to be his mother and James, Joseph, Simon and Judas his brothers? Aren't his sisters our neighbors? Where did he get all this?"

Matthew 13:54–55

The people of Nazareth did not accept Jesus as the Messiah precisely because he and his family were so ordinary. Joseph, after all, was the village carpenter, and Mary was a homemaker, just like most of the other women. Yet it is out of this workaday environment that our redemption came.

How did being a carpenter or a homemaker further the coming of the Kingdom? Was Joseph a good craftsman, Mary a competent cook and housekeeper? Did Joseph join a craft guild? How would he have treated his employees? Did he always make enough to support his family? Was there ever a time when he couldn't find work? What did it mean to his career to have to flee to Egypt? Did he want his son to take over his business? Was he disappointed when Jesus did not? Did Mary resent being a homemaker? Did she take in work to help support the family? What did she do to support herself after Joseph died?

As I reflect on the daily work of the Holy Family, Lord, I must think about my own daily work in a new light. God can be found in the very act of working, if I am but willing to look there. My work is holy because it is a participation in God's ongoing creation of the world.

Jesus, Mary and Joseph, pray for me.

Awareness that people's work is a participation in God's activity ought to permeate, as the Second Vatican Council teaches, even "the most ordinary everyday activities. For while providing the substance of life for themselves and their families, men and women are performing their activities in a way which appropriately benefits society. They can justly consider that by their labor, they are unfolding the Creator's work, consulting the advantages of their brothers and sisters, and contributing by their personal industry to the realization in history of the divine plan."

John Paul II
Laborem Exercens

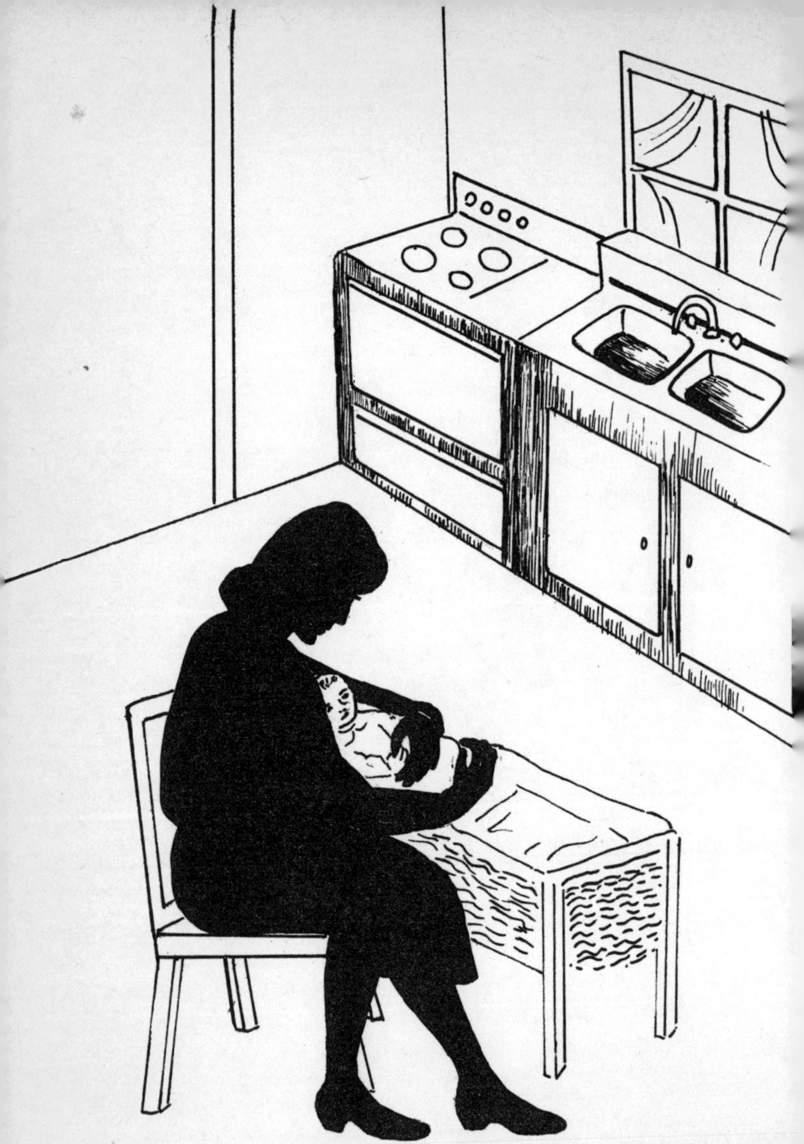

2

Raising a Family

As they were returning at the end of the feast, the child Jesus remained behind unknown to his parents. Thinking he was in the party, they continued their journey for a day, looking for him among their relatives and acquaintances.

Luke 2:43–44

What parents have not feared losing their child in a crowd? Joseph and Mary were not immune to the trials and tribulations of parenthood. They sat up at night with Jesus when he was ill, worked with him on his lessons, dreamed together about his future. And at the end, when it all seemed for naught, Mary stood at the foot of the cross and cried as she watched her son die.

How did Mary and Joseph learn to raise children? Were there any difficulties between them as a couple that had to be worked out? Why did Jesus cause them anxiety, and how did they handle it? What was it like to raise a special and gifted child? How did the pressures of moving affect their family life? Did Joseph have a mid-life crisis? Did Mary go through a difficult menopause? Did the couple and their son have to care for their elderly relatives? Was there an extended Holy Family? If Joseph died when Jesus was still young, how did Mary cope as a single parent? How did Jesus react when, according to Mark, his relatives were "convinced he was out of his mind"?

As I think about my own family—both the one in which I was raised and the one in which I now live, I realize that raising a family is hard work. Just like the Holy Family, I can look for help and comfort for this task from my relatives and friends, my church, and my God. Thank you, Lord, for my family and help me to do a better job living and working with them.

Jesus, Mary and Joseph, pray for me.

It must be remembered and affirmed that the family constitutes one of the most important terms of reference for shaping the social and ethical order of human work. The teaching of the church has always devoted special attention to this question. . . . In fact, the family is simultaneously a community made possible by work and the first school of work, within the home, for every person.

John Paul II
Laborem Exercens

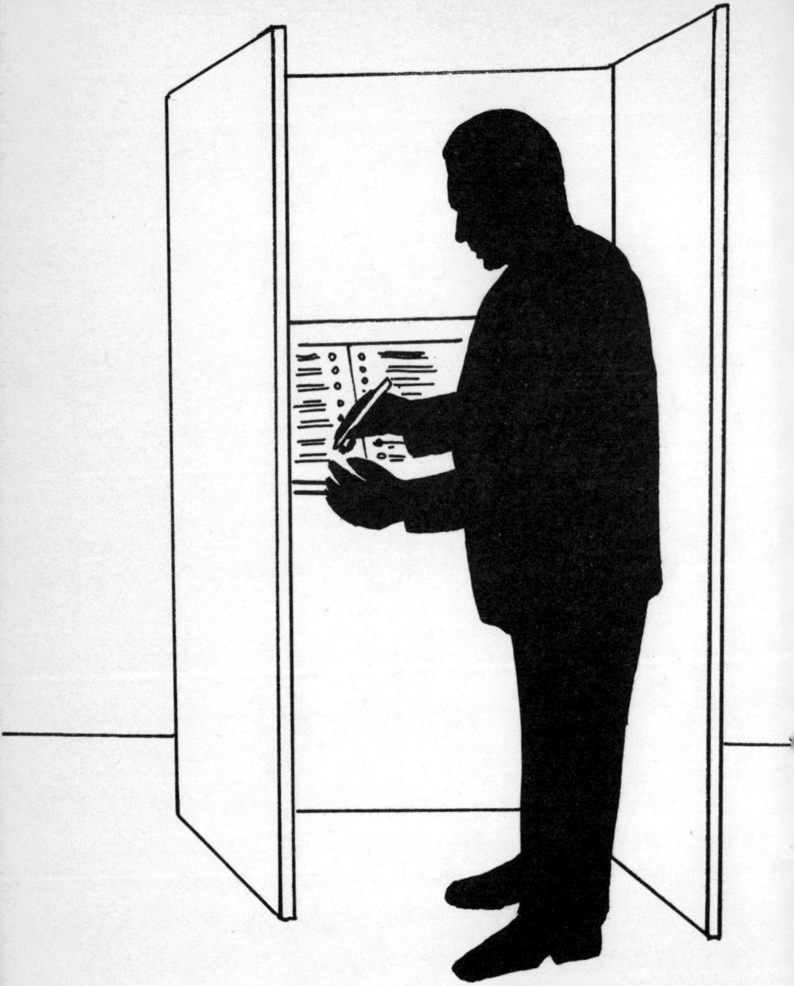

3

Being a Good Citizen

In those days Caesar Augustus published a decree ordering a census of the whole world. This first census took place while Quirinius was governor of Syria. Everyone went to register, each to his own town. And so Joseph went from the town of Nazareth in Galilee to Judea, to David's town of Bethlehem—because he was of the house and lineage of David—to register with Mary, his espoused wife, who was with child.

Luke 2:1–5

It is not enough to do one's job well and be a good family member. Like Joseph and Mary, Christians must also fulfill their responsibility to be participating and contributing members of society. This may mean voting in elections, being involved in neighborhood, community, national or international organizations, or volunteering for a good cause.

Why did Mary and Joseph agree to obey the decree of the hated Caesar? At what point did they decide it was necessary for them to disobey and flee the civil authorities? How did they function in Egypt as (probably) illegal aliens? Were they active in the village government in Nazareth? Did they pay their taxes? How did they feel about supporting the Roman military? Did Mary become a fugitive from "justice" after the crucifixion of her son? What are we to make of Jesus' ambivalent statements regarding civic duty ("Render unto Caesar the things that are Caesar's . . .")?

I know, Lord, that I have not done enough to make the world a better place for all people. Despite the fact that working in the public arena often seems overwhelming or useless, I need to be involved in some way. Please help me to learn to become a good and productive citizen, as I am sure the members of the Holy Family tried to be, even if it means protesting what is going on.

Jesus, Mary and Joseph, pray for me.

> For all who profess Christianity promise and give assurance that they will contribute as far as they can to the advancement of civil institutions. They must also strive with all their might not only that human dignity suffer no dishonor, but also, by the removal of every kind of obstacle, that all those forces be promoted which are conducive to moral living and contribute to it.
>
> John XXIII
> *Mater et Magistra*

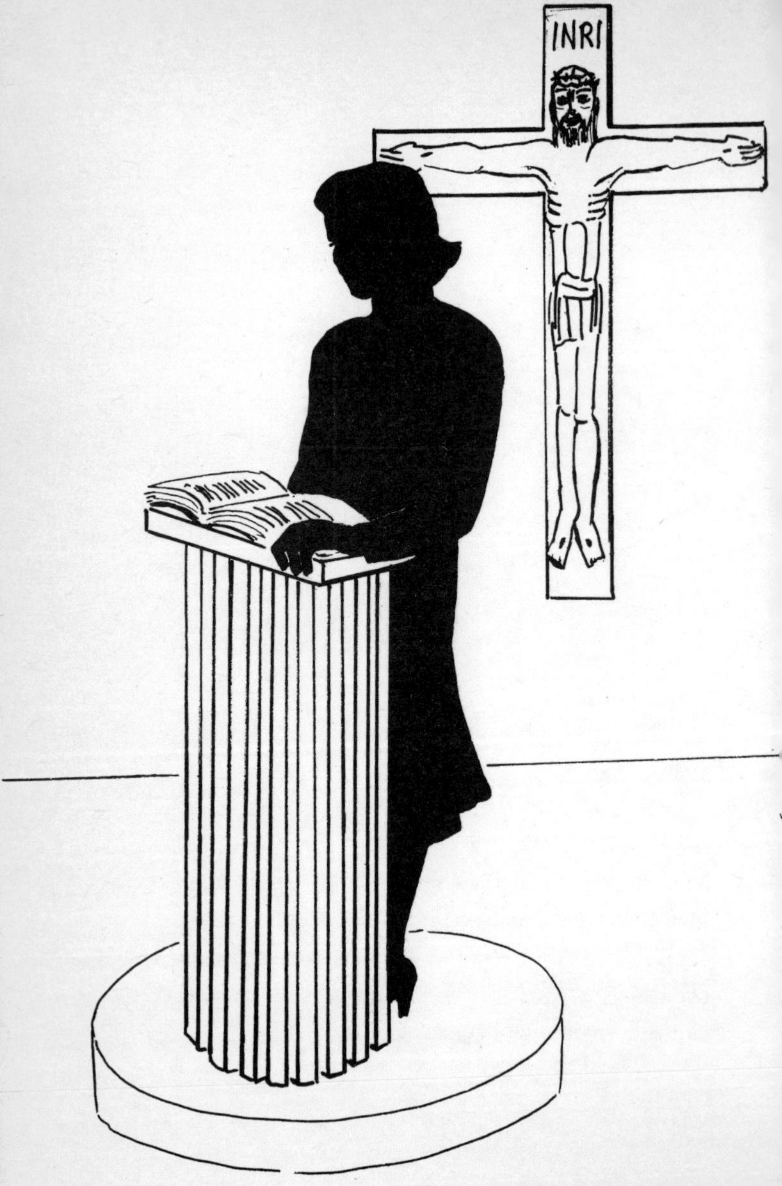
INRI

4

Practicing Religion

When the day came to purify them according to the law of Moses, the couple brought him up to Jerusalem so that he could be presented to the Lord, for it is written in the law of the Lord, "Every first-born male shall be consecrated to the Lord."

Luke 2:22–23

Being an active member of a church is never an easy task. It often entails its own form of hard work. At times, it must have been a burden for Joseph, Mary, and Jesus to follow the strict prescriptions of the Jewish Law. Yet their religion was obviously a source of strength for them and central to their lives—as it can be to ours.

What did it mean to be a practicing Jew in the first century? Was Joseph an elder in the Nazareth synagogue? Did Mary belong to the women's group? Was Jesus bar-mitzvahed? What did they think about the various reform movements in Judaism (such as the Pharisees and the Essenes)? How did they react when their kinsman John began to take on the religious establishment? Did Jesus go to rabbinical school? Was he rebellious there? What did his parents think of his radical ideas? Did either of them think that their son would become the foundation of an entirely new religion?

Practicing my religion is part of my daily work. I have both a right and a duty to help make my church an effective instrument of God's will, and in return I owe the church my allegiance and support. Lord, let me follow in the footsteps of the Holy Family as an active and faithful member of my church.

Jesus, Mary and Joseph, pray for me.

> Wherever the Church is present, there individuals are reborn or resurrected in Christ. Those who are thus reborn or who have risen again in Christ feel themselves oppressed by no external force. Rather, realizing they have achieved perfect liberty, they freely move toward God. Hence, whatever is seen by them as good and morally right, that they approve and put into effect.
>
> John XXIII
> *Mater et Magistra*

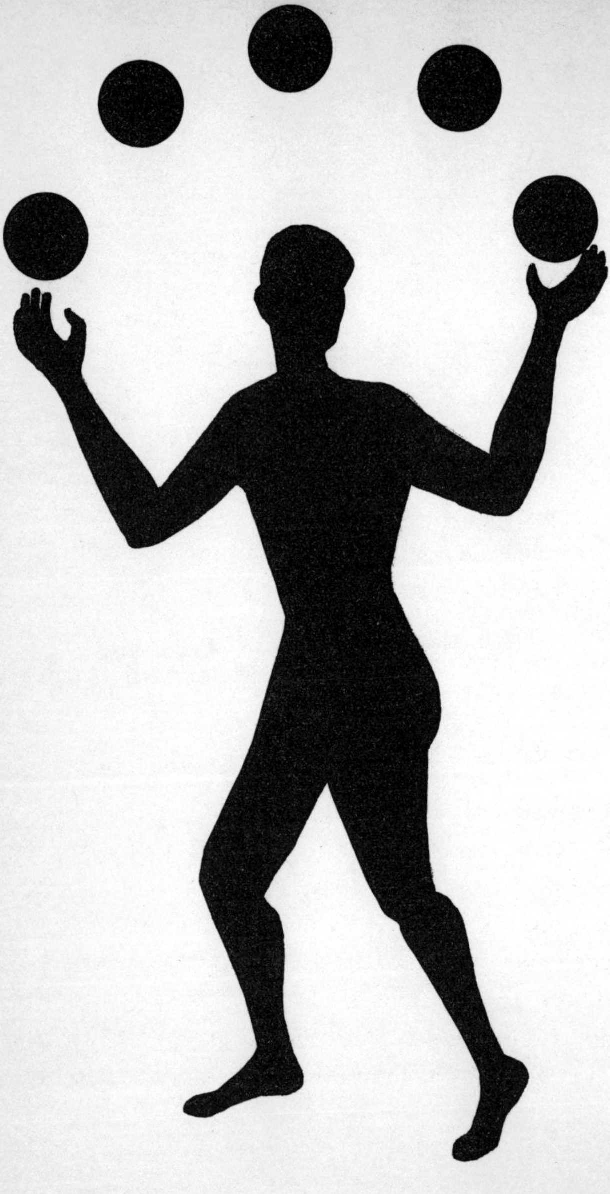

5

Balancing Responsibilities

My Father is at work until now, and I am at work as well.

John 5:17

Work is part of the human condition and entails more than just paid employment. It includes all the productive activity that helps bring about the reign of God on earth: on our jobs, with our families, in our communities and churches. In that sense, our work—like that of the Father, the Son, and the Spirit—is never done. Sometimes, however, the various spheres of our work are in conflict, and we must learn to balance our many responsibilities.

Why did Jesus stay behind in the temple when he was 12-years-old and cause his parents such anguish? What was the point at which the Holy Family ceased to obey the civil or religious authorities? Why was Jesus so harsh on family loyalty ("Let the dead bury the dead . . ."). Was Joseph a "workaholic"? Did Mary shy away from speaking her mind in public? Did Jesus work as a carpenter while he studied to be a rabbi? How did the Holy Family integrate work, family, citizenship and religion?

Keeping my daily work in balance is a lot like juggling a set of balls. Help me, Lord, to keep them all in the air, so that I give to each part of my work life the attention it deserves. May I remember that I am most near you when my life is whole and integrated.

Jesus, Mary and Joseph, pray for me.

> We have inherited from past generations and we have benefitted from the work of our contemporaries: for this reason, we have obligations towards all and we cannot refuse to interest ourselves in those who will come after us to enlarge the human family. The reality of human solidarity, which is a benefit for us, also imposes a duty.
>
> Paul VI
> *Populorum Progressio*

Other Books on the Spirituality of Work

- *Of Human Hands:*
  A Reader in the Spirituality of Work **$8.95**
  edited by Gregory A. Pierce

- *Caretakers of Creation:*
  Farmers Reflect on Their Faith and Work **$8.95**
  by Patrick Slattery

- *Precious Jewel Person:*
  Reflections on the Spirituality of Everyday Life .. **$8.95**
  by Barbara Ritter Garrison

- *Confident and Competent:*
  A Challenge for the Lay Church **$4.95**
  by William Droel and Gregory A. Pierce

- *The Spirituality of Work: Homemakers* **$2.95**
  by William Droel

- *The Spirituality of Work: Lawyers* **$2.95**
  by William Droel

- *The Spirituality of Work: Nurses* **$2.95**
  by William Droel

- *The Spirituality of Work: Teachers* **$2.95**
  by William Droel

Available from your Christian bookseller or call 800-397-2282.